BORN THIS WAY

Real Stories of Growing Up Gay

by
PAUL VITAGLIANO
(DJ Paul V.)

QUIRK
BOOKS

QUIRK
BOOKS

This book is dedicated to my wonderful mom, Irene, (may she rest in peace) and my sisters Andrea and Linda, and everyone who has shared their stories with me and with the world.

Library of Congress Cataloging in Publication Number: 2011946059

ISBN: 978-1-59474-599-7

Printed in China
Typeset in Eames Century Modern, Memphis and Neutra

Designed by Sugar
Production management by John J. McGurk

Quirk Books
215 Church Street
Philadelphia, PA 19106
quirkbooks.com

10 9 8 7 6 5 4 3 2 1

introduction

I am one of millions of out, proud gay people who didn't choose to be gay—I was born this way! I knew by age five that I felt a certain attraction to other boys, but I couldn't describe my feelings. Like many of my generation in the 1970s, I dated girls through high school to fit in, but it never felt natural. I came out to myself at nineteen. At thirty, when I sat my mother down for the "Mom, I have something to tell you" speech, she didn't blink and said, "Are you going to tell me you're gay?" I don't think I ever hugged her harder than I did that day. The truth is, our moms always know, even if they don't admit it right away. For me, the hardest part of growing up was feeling like I was the only gay person on the planet and had no one to talk to about it.

I started the Born This Way project to show young gay kids that they're not alone: many others have gone through everything they're experiencing now. We must share our stories and pay it forward for future generations. Being gay is as normal and natural as being straight. It is not a choice or a phase, it's not something you learn, and it's certainly not something that can or should be "cured" or "fixed." All children need love and nurturing and support. And there are so many great resources now for both children and adults, such as PFLAG, GLSEN, The Trevor Project, and It Gets Better. Use those tools and information to talk, communicate, and listen.

Inside this book, you'll find stories and photos about growing up gay in all kinds of families, everywhere from London to Mexico City. You'll find every shade of masculine and feminine, and yes, even some stereotypes. What you *won't* find is the shame that society places on those traits, only self-pride and self-acceptance. Not every boy who plays with dolls or every girl who plays with trucks—or exhibits gender-opposite behavior—is gay. But you will see that most of the kids in this book knew they were gay at an early age. These children have grown up to be doctors, lawyers, musicians, makeup artists, painters, and poets. They're now mothers, fathers, and loving partners. And they've all made invaluable contributions to the fabric of society.

In the six decades represented in this book, many have gone on to achieve great levels of success in their respective fields. I've included some of these famous faces of the LGBTQ community to help inspire today's gay youth to strive for their own greatness. Representative **Barney Frank** (1953) is the first openly gay member of the U.S. Congress and a progressive champion for human rights. Michael Musto (1964) is a television personality and writer known for his column in *The Village Voice*. Marc Shaiman (1967) is a Tony, Grammy, and Emmy Award winning composer. Actor/comedian **Patrick Bristow** (1968) has appeared on *Ellen*, *Seinfeld*, and *Curb Your Enthusiasm*. Photographer **Mike Ruiz** (1968) has shot for *Vanity Fair*, *Elle*, and *Vogue*. Steven Kirkham (1969) is Miss Perfidia, whose wig styling is seen everywhere from *Strangers with Candy* to *The Pee Wee Herman Show* on Broadway for HBO. Actor/comedian Frank DeCaro (1969) hosts "The Frank DeCaro Show" on Sirius XM Satellite Radio's OutQ 108l. **Billy Brasfield** (1970), aka **Billy B.** is one of the world's most sought-after makeup artists and a featured judge on *Ru Paul's Drag Race*.

Musician **Andy Bell** (1970) is lead singer of Erasure and an ambassador for New York's Hetrick-Martin Institute, which provides resources for LGBTQ youth. **Kent Fuher** (1971) is drag superstar Jackie Beat, and a featured columnist for *Frontiers IN LA* magazine. Jeffrey Schwarz (1977) is an acclaimed producer and filmmaker. Sia Fuller (1978) is a Grammy nominated singer-songwriter. **Bill Coleman** (1979) is a club DJ, writer, and music supervisor whose record label features LGBTQ recording artists Cazwell, Amanda Lepore, and the Ones. Clinton Leupp (1979) is activist and drag performer Miss Coco Peru, whose films include *To Wong Foo, Thanks for Everything! Julie Newmar*. The Lane Twins, Gary and Larry (1980) created the award-winning documentary *Hollywood to Dollywood*, which chronicles their coming-out story and meeting their idol, Dolly Parton. Sutan Amrull (1982), aka **Raja Gemini**, is a renowned makeup artist, drag performer, and the Season 3 winner of *Ru Paul's Drag Race*. **Perez Hilton** (1983) is a world-famous celebrity blogger.

Writer Noah Michelson (1985) is the editor of Gay Voices at the Huffington Post. Journalist Matt Baume (1987) documents the fight for marriage equality at Stop8.org. And Kevin Farrell (1990) cofounded the popular Unicorn Booty website to keep the LGBTQ community connected with pop culture and gay activism. I am thrilled and honored to have all of them included here. But these are only a handful of our many success stories.

We are all here to say to the LGBTQ youth of today: **You are a gift to this world.** Never let those who bully or taunt you prevent you from being exactly who you are. Yes, it can be tough, and the bullying situation in our schools is something we must work to stop. But your teen years are a mere nanosecond compared to the decades of happiness, joy, and love that will come into your life as a proud, gay adult. This world needs what you add to it, so I implore you never to consider taking your own life. If my book prevents even one life lost, I consider myself blessed.

My closing message is to parents: Understand that your child might be straight or they might be gay—and that's OK! So, please, love *all* your children unconditionally, and nurture and encourage what makes them happy and healthy. Raise them to accept and respect all people, no matter the differences. Teach them that what defines them are their actions and deeds and not their sexuality. And above all—no matter the gender—teach them that love is love.

— **Paul V.**

bernie, age 4

One Halloween, our mother dressed up my brother
Dennis (*left*, age 3) and me (*right*) as Carmen Miranda, a
Hollywood star noted for her signature fruited turban.
Most boys this young dressed as cowboys and pirates,
and I can't imagine that we asked to dress this way. But
apparently we cooperated—lipstick and rouge to boot!—
and we look happy.

I went through grammar school without a girlfriend, but
in high school I did the requisite amount of dating. On
dates, I'd often find the waiter more attractive than the
girl I was with. By my early twenties, I was going to gay
bars in Chicago. My brother came out to me, and it wasn't
long after that our parents learned they had two gay sons.

My brother Dennis had a wonderful life. But he was gone
too soon, cut down by AIDS in 1993. At his memorial
service, I made reference to this picture, wondering
aloud about my mother: "What was she thinking?" The
audience, my mother and father included, couldn't help
but laugh.

I don't think my mother knew in 1948 what the future
held for her sons, nor do I think our Carmen Miranda
costumes made us gay. But it was still a momentous
beginning, don't you think?

1940   1950   1960   1970

1948

Chicago, Illinois

1953

Bayonne, New Jersey

barney, age 13

I had a normal and happy life growing up, with a strong family and many friends. I was good in school and enjoyed playing sports. I went to a big public high school, and luckily I was never picked on or bullied.

I remember, when I was about eleven, some boys were passing around playing cards with naked women on them, and I just had no reaction to them at all. At first I thought I was asexual, but I soon realized I just had an opposite attraction, to boys.

I remember very clearly that at age thirteen, during some horseplay with my male friends, it finally dawned on me that I was gay. I was terrified and frightened and discouraged, and I figured I would deal with it simply by never telling anybody. Thinking back, I knew I had those feelings as young as age five, but I didn't realize it at the time.

Because I was closeted until 1987, I had difficulty leading a so-called normal life. I was in hiding. Since coming out, I've found everything I need to live a happy life. Come out as soon as you can. I can't think of any people I've known who've said their life got worse after coming out. The consequences are almost always better than people think they'll be, and the negatives are much less. If you can't fully come out, find other gay and lesbian people and socialize with them, and find other people you can trust with your truth. Being who you are and being happy with yourself—those are the most important things in life.

robert, age 3

I have always been an avid record collector. In kindergarten, my teacher told my father that **I liked to play with the girls and their dolls.** My dad did not like that at all. So he taught me the "boy stuff," like throwing a football. In junior high, the other boys did not want me on their teams, and I was called a sissy by most of them. My eighth-grade teacher even said to me, "Robert, are you a faggot?" The boys in my class called me "Rob-Butt" and **I was bullied and ridiculed by the older, larger boys.** So I kept to myself. Things got a little better in high school. By then, most of the bullies had failed their classes, but I graduated at seventeen. I came out to my parents when I was nineteen, and since then I have been out and proud, even while serving in the Marine Corps Reserve program. **Life improves once we are open and honest about being gay.**

1940   1950   1960   1970

maureen, age 9

I'm here on the right with my BFF, Cheryl. We're snuggled up together, and we used to hug and kiss every time we met. At our age in that era, people thought it was cute, but I really loved her. I asked my folks if we could adopt her, even though she had her own parents. In the 1950s, no one used the word *gay* yet, and I had no idea what a homosexual was. But I knew my love for Cheryl felt wonderful.

1957
Upstate New York

1940 1950 1960 1970

jerome, age 8

We didn't have the word *gay* when I was a child, only the word *sissy*. Thanks to my older sister's 1950s movie magazines, I was obsessed with Hollywood glamour. In this photo, I'm emulating Marilyn Monroe, Jayne Mansfield, or Mamie Van Doren—perhaps all three! Growing up "special" in a tiny, rural Texas town wasn't easy, but I survived. Through the years, I cringed whenever I came across this photo. But now, some fifty years after it was taken, I find it charming. Self-acceptance at last!

1959
Groesbeck,
Texas

1940   1950   1960   1970

felix, age 5

A couple years after this photo was taken, **the birds-and-the-bees story circulated around the playground.** My first reaction was to suggest to my best friend a position I demonstrated with my hands. I made two peace signs and connected them, also known as a "scissor sister." And I said, "Well, couldn't we just—?" Her reaction made it quite clear: "No. We cannot."

1940   1950   1960   1970

frank, age 5

My mother always said that I was a smiling and laughing child. Everywhere she took me, people would remark, **"What a wonderful laughing baby."** She tells me that I soon learned that smiling—and sometimes posing— would open doors for me. In first grade, I held other boys' hands and pretended to be married to them. I was forbidden to play with dolls, but I still managed to sew outfits for my sister's Barbies. **I hid my sewn creations in a bag and buried them in the yard** so that I could bring them out to play whenever my parents left the house. In school, I endured beatings and humiliation. When the school bell rang at 3:00 in the afternoon to go home, I bolted out the door to avoid the bullies who waited to humiliate me in the hallways. As for the man I am today? I was born this way, and I am proud!

1950   1960   1970   1980

liz, age 6

My mother had to bribe me to wear a dress, and I insisted on no puffed sleeves or ruffles of any kind. I was obsessed with all things NASA and wanted to be an astronaut. **I would lie upside down in our living room chairs and pretend I was orbiting Planet Earth in my own rocket.**

When I developed a huge crush on my butch gym teacher (didn't we all?), my mother told me that crushes on other girls were perfectly normal. I spent a lot of time being "perfectly normal" at summer camp, with crushes on older campers and cute, butch counselors. None of my crushes materialized into anything more than long, flowery letters professing undying friendship. I dated boys because that was just what you did. It wasn't until my senior year that I finally came to terms with my gayness. **I knew I wanted more from another woman than long, flowery letters.**

1961
Buffalo,
New York

1950   1960   1970   1980

1961
Chianciano Terme, Italy

marco, age 6

This photo was taken at a café in an Italian spa town. My mom, dad, brother, and I all sat down in these modern 1960s chrome chairs; however, I was the only one who crossed my legs in such a flirtatious way! As children, we almost never censor ourselves.

I am certain that nobody *becomes* homosexual, and many of our childhood behaviors, mannerisms, and choices are revealing. Seeing this picture now, I think, "Wasn't it so obvious that I was gay from the beginning?" My mother asked me about it during my twenties, but I didn't actually admit it to her until I was forty-five. To my surprise, she was very happy and said, "I wish you knew you could have told me before." I am so glad I got to tell her before she died. It is important to show who you really are without fear, because your photos will always show it anyway.

1950   1960   1970   1980

claudia, age 5

In grade school, I had an imaginary girlfriend. **I wouldn't allow anyone to sit with me on the school bus so that my imaginary girlfriend could sit next to me.** The word *lesbian* didn't exist where I grew up. I did not come out until I was twenty-two, and I fought it tooth and nail. In my mind, it would mean that I was abnormal. I give the gay teens today a lot of credit for coming out so young and realizing exactly who they are.

1962
Ravenna,
Ohio

1950   1960   1970   1980

mark, age 16

The most intense day in high school was the day I tried to explain to my best friend that I was upset he spent so much time with his girlfriend. Our friendship became awkward from then on. Lots of things happened that I should've realized were gay signs, but there was so little information back then. I simply thought that if I stayed religious, I would outgrow those mystery feelings. This photo of me is my favorite, since being the piano player at age sixteen kept me popular enough to be included. But I always felt that I was alone somehow. My life bloomed when I came out, and my partner and I have been together over twenty years.

1950　　　　1960　　　　1970　　　　1980

ed, age 2

This photo shows a boy who just won't stop being happy. It shows I have a spirit that refuses to quit. Growing up, one of the biggest challenges for me was asserting my individuality. After a long, drawn-out process, I finally came out to myself in college. I realized I needed to be far away from home to really become my true self. Coming out to my family was incredibly painful. It was the early '80s, and my father said he wouldn't even drink out of the same glass as me because I'm gay. He's mellowed a bit since then, but we aren't very close. I wish we were closer. Somehow, I've been able to keep seeing that happy kid inside myself, and that has kept me going.

1962

Peoria,
Illinois

1950   1960   1970   1980

sam, age 8

Here I am in my cha-cha costume after winning first place with my partner at a talent show. **This particular pose has seemed to follow me in photos throughout my life.** I was always wearing costumes or hamming it up for the camera. I loved twirling around the living room in a long, ruffled, hot pink gown my mom had for dress-up time. Though I was the only boy in my dance class, I got along fabulously with all the girls.

1950   1960   1970   1980

jeffrey, age 4

What I remember most about this pose is that it made
my father uncomfortable, and he tried to hurry the photo
being taken. **But looking at this picture today, I have to
say I love it!**

1950   1960   1970   1980

kevin, age 4

I'm originally from a small town in Nebraska. At the time this photo was taken, I was joyful, giddy, fearless, and ready to perform. I mean, who wouldn't want to dance around on stage and receive all that attention? I remember being especially excited to see the older girls with their fire batons. But my baton lessons lasted only one summer. After that I started to get the message that boys don't twirl the baton or play with Barbie dolls. It wasn't until I was twenty that I embraced my sexual identity. It took me a long time to get comfortable with this photo, but now I look at it with great affection.

1964
Cozad, Nebraska

1964

Brooklyn, New York

michael, age 9

I was that rarity, an only child born to an Italian American family in Brooklyn. Practically from birth, I retreated into a wall of shyness. I knew I was different—more sensitive, let's say—than most of the kids in the neighborhood, but I wasn't sure just what that meant.

In 1964, my cousin introduced me to the music of Diana Ross and the Supremes, the glittery, arm-gesturing Motown girl group, and that was transformative. It also gave me something to bond with another male over. But that wasn't sexual. That came later, in 1966, when a loin-clothed hottie named Ron Ely hit the small screen as Tarzan. That's when I knew I was gay, because I couldn't wait to watch the show every week. And when Diana Ross and the Supremes were guest stars on it, I was in gay heaven!

Despite these coded diversions, I never knew if there was a future for me as a gay man. There were no out role models and precious little positive information at the time. In fact, homosexuality was considered a disorder! But I hung in there and eventually moved across the bridge to Manhattan, where I found a thriving, creative community that I still belong to. Today, I'm the gayest person on Earth. And I still know every last one of those Supremes' arm gestures.

1950   1960   1970   1980

keith, age 2

Believe it or not, I remember the moment captured in my photo. It was when I saw *him*, a dreamy teenage friend of our family. I didn't feel gay or different at this moment, just in love. And I'm so glad I'm dressed quite handsomely in my tie, plaid vest, and penny loafers. I suppose it was around age five that I sensed I was different, as I heard my parents arguing about the clothes and toys my mother was buying me. Not to mention my constant desire to fly like Mary Poppins or the Flying Nun, which drove my father nuts. The ability to fly away, if even just in my imagination, helped me get through it all.

1964

Detroit, Michigan

1950 1960 1970 1980

jeffrey, age 3

I was a smart, eccentric kid who was prone to dramatic moments. The best thing my parents did for me was getting me involved in a local community theater program to channel my creative energy. Growing up, I couldn't understand why I didn't like football, dating, or other things Texan. It was not until I went off to college that my first "girlfriend" suspected what was going on, labeled me as gay, and got me on the path to self-discovery.

1950   1960   1970   1980

1967
Scotch Plains, New Jersey

marc, age 8

The earliest memory I have of understanding that I liked boys was staring at the *Meet The Beatles!* album cover with my sister and knowing I too thought Paul McCartney was the cute one. My first boy crushes happened at summer camp, over some of the older boys or a camp counselor or two. Then a few neighborhood friends and some cute jocks at school and fellow actors in the community theater and ...oh, well, I guess I had a lot of crushes.

My only distinct memory of being bullied is when a male friend of my sister's wrote FAG on a piece of sheet music in my room. I remember my father taped a similarly colored piece of paper on top to cover up the hateful word. And I remember I felt worse for my father than I did for myself.

I was always out to everyone but my parents. I am embarrassed by how long I kept the additional "roommate decoy" bed in the living room for when my parents visited me. Much to my mother's credit, when I told her of another friend who'd died of AIDS, she asked me if Scott and I were "more than roommates." I've been with my partner, Scott, for thirty-three years now. Although we do not have children, we share a song-writing career that has given birth to many proud accomplishments. I have never had a day in my life when I didn't feel it was a blessing being born gay.

todd, age 4

I've seen home movies of me as a small boy, fearlessly singing and dancing for the family. My parents thought I had enough charisma to be on television, so they took me to Hollywood to get some headshots done. All I can remember is that I was breathless traveling to Tinseltown. I was sure that we would run into Ginger from *Gilligan's Island*. We didn't see Ginger, but I did meet Grandpa Munster (aka Al Lewis) at Universal Studios. I cried for hours because he was green and old and kissed me on the cheek. Putting that tragedy behind me, I continued to perform and got my big break at an audition for Ron Moody's production of *Oliver*. Walking into the Ahmanson Theater in downtown Los Angeles and seeing all the other little boys who loved to sing and dance, I thought I was in heaven.

1967
Hollywood, California

1950   1960   1970   1980

patrick, age 6

I knew by no later than age four that I had a secret. By age ten, I had full knowledge that I was what everyone else seemed to hate. I tried to pass for straight until college, where I found others like myself. The stress created by years of hiding was replaced by a deep spiritual sigh of relief when I came out in 1981. **My family's reaction was akin to. "Yeah, we know. Now pass the butter and get your elbows off the table."**

mike, age 4

I knew I was gay pretty early on, from about the age of five. As a kid, I was captivated by Patrick Duffy on TV's *Man from Atlantis*. He was always in his little swim trunks and was quite buff back then. He also had webbed hands and toes, which were some kind of odd turn-on for me.

Growing up in a blue-collar, intolerant environment in the suburbs of Montreal, I wasn't exposed to a lot of progressive thinking. Especially in my early teens, I sure could have used a helping hand along the way. I stayed in the closet until the ripe old age of seventeen, when I just couldn't contain myself anymore. At which point, I came out screaming and flailing my arms.

At the age of twenty, I moved to the United States with just three hundred dollars in my pocket and a desire to be involved in the entertainment world. I'm now based in Manhattan, and doing just that.

steven, age 4

My sister remembers this as her baton-twirling costume.
I don't remember wearing it, but I'm sure my mom
thought it was harmless and funny. As early as this age,
I loved feminine things, art, and playing doctor with
my cute neighbors. Later I was in chorus and band, like
many of us back then. And I was the only boy in junior
high to choose disco class over football.

When *The Rocky Horror Picture Show* played at the
local theater, I went done up as Frank-N-Furter and
dethroned the person playing him. I realized that if
I was performing, I was more powerful. In the '80s I
discovered Hollywood and other out-of-the-closet gay
teens. I had my first gay kiss at an under-eighteen disco
called the Odyssey Club in West Hollywood. We all loved
Boy George and the freedom to cross gender barriers.

In 1985 I moved to New York City and became part of
the nightlife. Drag culture had taken over Manhattan
nightclubs, and I morphed into a new romantic drag
queen. Within a year, I was hired by Patricia Field as a
stylist. I won a drag contest at the Boy Bar club as Miss
Perfidia in 1986. I lived with established drag performers
who trained me well, and I took my show all over the
world. My talent with wigs eventually led to Broadway
and television work.

1969
Carlsbad, California

frank, age 7

As a kid, I dressed like Charles Nelson Reilly, I had posters of David Cassidy on my bedroom wall, and I owned my own food processor by the time I was fifteen! My father, God love him, tried his best to interest me in pursuits more traditionally masculine than shopping and reading *Redbook*.

My classmates certainly knew I was gay. I was called a fag every day from the sixth grade on. I was a quadruple-whammy teasing target, too. I wasn't just effeminate—I was a fat, four-eyed, straight-A student whom teachers adored. The worst experience was in art class. I made a giant psychedelic letter F out of cardboard and tempera paint. It was just like the M on the wall on *The Mary Tyler Moore Show*. My teacher held it up in class and one kid shouted, "What's the *F* for? Faggot?!" The class howled. I was devastated and, worst of all, I did nothing. I wasn't yet ready to admit I was gay. I finally came out right before my seventeenth birthday, beginning a relationship with a boy in my geometry class. From our first mall date, I was ready to sign the bridal registry. Oh, what a sexy summer we shared before going off to college. I'm proud to say that we still send each other birthday cards.

Today, my husband and I are nearing the sixteen-year mark of being together. No matter the awful things my mother said when I first came out to her—and there were some doozies!—she left me with some good advice. "Nobody is better than you, and you're no better than anyone else." Those are some pretty fabulous words to live by, whether you're gay or not.

◆

1969
Little Falls, New Jersey

joe, age 7

I was an effeminate boy who liked to play house and lip-sync to Cher songs. I would put my sister's black tights over my head, throw back the legs like long hair, and sing "Half-Breed" into a hairbrush! My parents were not okay with this.

I felt terrible, knowing that I wasn't like other boys. Although **I kept my sexuality quiet**, other boys (and the girls) could see that I was different, and I was bullied. I was constantly called hateful names. I was spit on, pushed around, and punched. Unlike many gay boys, **I told my parents about the bullying**. They came to the school and told the teachers and principals, but nothing changed. I became isolated and depressed at age fourteen, and my mother took me to therapy, which saved my life. The therapist was open to hearing about my real thoughts, fantasies, and identity. He taught me how to **fight back against those bullies with my words**, and it worked. He also inspired me to become a therapist as an adult. There is help out there.

1970
Oak Park,
Michigan

billy, age 7

I was a creative momma's boy, and I sucked my thumb
until I was thirteen. When I played house with my cousins
and my sister, I was always a "girl" with a towel on my
head, pretending I had long hair. I remember always
feeling like an oddball, misfit, or less than good enough.
In sixth grade, we were assigned to draw a picture of our
teacher sitting at her desk. My teacher didn't like mine
and she made fun of it in front of the entire class, and
I was devastated. My mom picked me up from school
and I began to cry. When I told her the story, she did a
screeching U-turn in the street and bolted us back to the
school principal's office. They called the teacher in, and my
mother read her like a cheap novel! My mother has always
had my back, and she still does now at age eighty.

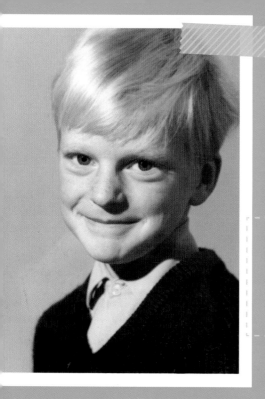

andy, age 5

Basically, I felt like a girl—or an overly sensitive boy
with a very vivid imagination. We would put on shows in
the garden, and I did drag brilliantly in my sister's long
party dress. I think I was quite scared of the other boys
my age, and by age ten, I was called a sissy and a poofter
before I even knew what it all meant. The milkman once
said to me, "Andy, why do you walk like a girl?" This
really screwed me up for a while, and I'd think, "Well,
how does a girl walk, anyway?"

1960   1970   1980   1990

brett, age 7

Here I am in my Easter finery sitting next to my
beautiful mother. Please note the scowl on my face. I
am furious—*furious!*—that I am adorned with that plain
white carnation, the most blasé of boutonnieres, while
Mother is wearing the most *gorgeous* violet corsage I have
ever seen. We were all preparing to go to Mass when the
flowers came out, and I pitched a fit about it. I skulked
through the Easter Sunday service and possibly even
after we got home. I guess I learned early on that life is
not always fair.

1970
Lima, Ohio

grant, age 6

There was a page in our family photo album of six-year-old me dressed in all sorts of drag: an oversized gown, a flamenco dress, beehive wigs—all worn with a big smile. In my teens, **I frantically tore this page out and shredded the images** to dispel suspicions that I might be a homo. I was terrified that if anyone found out my secret, I would be utterly destroyed. I did whatever it took (dating girls, playing football) to stay below the radar. **By age twenty-five, I felt like a dam with a thousand cracks**, and I finally came out to my friends and family. It was the best move that I ever made.

Today I live in New York City with the love of my life (my husband of five years) and our two dogs. I wouldn't change a thing, but I *do* wish I still had those great photos. Last year I found one stray drag photo in my parents' attic, and now it's proudly framed in our apartment for all to see. It's a daily reminder to be true to yourself, that **there is no "normal,"** and what you fear most in yourself can one day become your greatest gift and source of strength.

kent, age 8

In homage to my mom's Italian heritage, my dad turned our boring suburban backyard into a beautiful oasis with Roman columns and replicas of classical statues. When my sister suggested I give Caesar a little kiss, I went for it!

1971
Scottsdale, Arizona

1960   1970   1980   1990

1972

Baton Rouge, Louisiana

andré, age 4

I recently came across this photo from Easter of 1972. In it, I'm holding a tiny purse that my grandma made from an old margarine container combined with her delicate crocheting. When I shared this photo with my mom, she remarked at how cute my little sister was. I pointed out that the photo was not of her daughter, but rather of her proud four-year-old son, and she silently turned the page. Growing up, my sexuality was the proverbial elephant in the room: it was always present, but never discussed.

In my twelve years of Catholic schooling, just about every report card included the comment, "André is a sensitive boy." That was Catholic-school code for "gay as a daisy." It was tough growing up sensitive, and the journey was never easy. But it was worth it, for I can now say that I love who I am and I love the life I've built for myself. I love that I've learned to honor and protect that sensitive little boy with the pink Easter purse and black galoshes.

I have a terrific job as a writer. I have a wonderful partner and a cozy home with three cats. It's exactly the kind of life I was told would never be an option for me.

◆

brian, age 5

One of my favorite activities was dancing in my grandmother's high heels. I would sneak into her closet and emerge in her black patent-leather pumps, my favorite pair. That's my little brother wearing those favorite black shoes. I was a little bossy as his dance instructor, saying, "Hey, do it this way. Step, two, three, four. Turn, two, three, four." My parents called me the Mother Hen. I love that I was always such a free spirit. I'm still a free spirit today, thanks in large part to the love and support of the women in my life, especially my mother and my grandmother.

1972
Columbus,
Ohio

arthur, age 4

In kindergarten, **I would chase and kiss my friend Kevin on the playground.** He didn't like it, and the other kids would tease him about it. But I didn't see anything wrong with it. These days this behavior would be called "not respecting boundaries."

1972

Hillsboro, Oregon

mark, age 7

As a sensitive and creative kid, **books were my refuge.**
I befriended a girl in first grade, and the unison shouts
of "sissy" intensified. So I basically had no friends in
school. Does this sound familiar? Then I met a boy
named John, another skinny teacher's pet. **With his
Coke-bottle glasses, he fit the geek stereotype I could
relate to**—and my lifelong pattern for romantic interests
was firmly set. But our intimate conversations weren't
allowed in class, and teachers kept us apart.

I attended six different schools in nine years' time, yet
the bullies always immediately pegged me as gay. I
was shoved and locked inside a gym locker for an hour
and got beat up for daring to wear pink, which put me
in the hospital with a dislocated jaw. If I sought help
I was told, "You brought this on yourself. Why can't
you act more like the other boys?" In college, while no
longer compelled to maintain secrecy or protect my
parents from worry, I fell apart and was overwhelmed
by depression. After another long period of self-imposed
solitude, **I finally found the strength to slowly rebuild
my life.** Thankfully, today I am surrounded by good
friends and loved ones.

1960　　　　1970　　　　1980　　　　1990

brian, age 5

I was quiet, sensitive, and nonathletic from the get-go, and I cared little for typical boy things, like playing outside, running, or throwing balls at people. I much preferred to watch television, color with crayons, or play with my collection of G.I. Joe, Ken, and *Six Million Dollar Man* dolls. It was right around second grade that I consciously trained myself never to show a dangling or limp wrist in public. And I learned early on that the best protection from mean boys was having a tough, fearless girl like my best friend Terri around me.

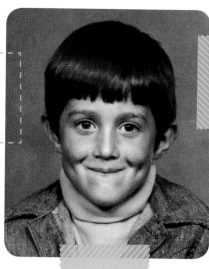

1973
Las Vegas, New Mexico

1973
Yellowstone,
Wyoming

tracy, age 7

Here I am, just out of first grade, on a family trip out
West. We lived in a suburb of Cleveland, Ohio, and spent
almost three weeks on the road. I remember how exciting
it was to get this cowboy hat and run around playing
cowboys and Indians (no, we weren't very politically
correct back then). Boys did not interest me in the least;
**I had my first serious crush on a girl in second grade,
and I never looked back.** When I was that young, I never
would have imagined that I could be married to a woman,
but I now live in New Hampshire and I am.

1960   1970   1980   1990

gabi, age 7

I didn't quit trying to be straight until age forty-five.
I met a woman during a visit to a mutual friend in the
United States, and we fell in love almost instantly. We
continued our long-distance relationship (and seventeen-
hour flights) for almost a year, seeing each other only
every few months. I split up with my then boyfriend,
and I came out in a long e-mail to about seventy people,
including my boss. The response was overwhelmingly
positive. I married my love in April 2010, and we now
live in the Netherlands, where gay people have the same
rights that straight people do.

1973

Lido di Jesolo,
Italy

henry, age 5

I'm Henry on the right, with my brother Rocky on the left. Our household told us that being gay was a sickness and that gays were defective. I suffered at the hands of shrinks, priests, and my mother trying to change me. **The one person who made all that truly bearable was my little brother, Rocky.** Growing up, I knew he was gay before I knew I was. And he always supported me with no judgments. He once cheered me up by performing "I'm Every Woman" by Chaka Khan in my mother's platform shoes. We were very different as boys. Rocky liked perfume, makeup, and glamour, whereas **I liked sweaty men, rock music, and leather. We still like the same things now.**

1960   1970   1980   1990

clarissa, age 4

I always wanted to be tough and dirty, and I would go to work with my dad the mechanic. My mom found a way to get me to wear dresses by making them herself, patterning them after Lucy Van Pelt of the *Peanuts* cartoon: I acknowledged Lucy's toughness, and **I felt tough in those dresses, too.**

1960   1970   1980   1990

chris, age 12

I hated Little League. While this baseball pic was being taken, I was being bullied by an older teammate for being a sissy and a fag. In hindsight, I wonder if he had a crush on me.

For years, my cheeks would burn with embarrassment when I looked back on my journal pages. I hated this gay boy: his girly script, his passion for Judy Garland, and his unabashed enthusiasm, which I came to see as effeminate. But now I love this boy so, so much. If I had a time machine, I'd go back and hold him tight and tell him he was wonderful and good and brave—and not to listen to anyone telling him otherwise.

1974

Albuquerque, New Mexico

1960   1970   1980   1990

rae, age 5

Seeing this picture of myself decked out in a dress makes me realize just how uncomfortable I was in girls' clothing. It was a nice feeling to be dressed up, but I would have been happier in a little suit and tie.

When I came out in 2009, the majority of my family's response was, "We have known forever; we just wanted you to be comfortable enough to tell us." None of them—including my own children—have bad feelings about me being a lesbian.

1974
Barstow,
California

1960   1970   1980   1990

DC, age 7

I remember asking my mom if she thought I had a good figure. She told me, "Little boys don't worry about their figures." Growing up in a small south Texas town in the 1970s, **I had no gay role models.** I didn't even know what being gay was. Yet people at school called me names. **How did they know I was gay before I did?**

I tried to tell my mom I was gay when I was in college, but I couldn't get the words out through the tears. She finished my sentence for me, and hugged me. "It doesn't matter to me one bit, sweetie," she said. "I'll tell Daddy, and **at least I know I'll always have someone to go shopping with.**"

1960   1970   1980   1990

dennis, age 3

I vaguely remember this picture being taken. It's still amazing to me that my pose here was not a clear sign to my parents. When I told them at the age of nineteen that I was gay, their reaction was less than supportive. In my family, like many Catholic families, we have an unwritten rule: If you don't talk about it, it will go away. They did not want to believe that this little boy, with his knee pointed just so and fabulous hands on his hips, grew up to be a gay man. Denial, anyone?

After I came out, various childhood pictures started to make sense to me. I'm proud to say that my picture was so incredibly gay that it actually inspired Paul V. to create his blog—and now this book—to help kids who may be struggling with coming out or being gay and, yes, to get a few good laughs along the way.

Today, I live in Long Beach, California, and I recently opened my own hair salon. Imagine that, a gay hairstylist. Weird, eh?

1974
Saint Louis, Missouri

dean, age 4

Back in the 1970s, the majority of us **grew up in an "Archie Bunker" atmosphere.** My parents were never afraid of using the N word or shy about talking about "the queers" who lived on the next block. I remember cringing every time they would start to talk about them, knowing that soon my truth had to come out or I'd have to run away to a place like Pleasure Island from *Pinocchio*.

Today I live in Hollywood and work as a successful makeup artist. I have done makeup on people like Beyoncé, Lady Gaga, and Mariah Carey, to name a few. And **I am living the life I always dreamed of.** I look back on the small stuff now and laugh, because I remember it seemed to be so all-consuming.

1975
Hollywood,
Florida

1960   1970   1980   1990

kelly jo, age 10

I didn't tell my mom it was school-photo day, and I dressed
myself. She had no idea until three months later, when
the large package of photos came in the mail and she saw
them. But **it was worth it to me to dress the way I felt most
comfortable.** As a little girl, the thought of being forced to
wear a dress gave me the cold sweats. I'm forty-five now, and
I still don't own a dress! When we're young we're told a lot
of things, such as how to act, what to do, what to believe, and
how to feel. Then with time we find out what really matters
to us. Yes, it was hard growing up gay. But, looking back
now, **I wouldn't change a thing.** It made me who I am today:
a strong, creative, and caring person.

1960   1970   1980   1990

amos, age 8

Who would've thought that this kid would be a lesbian? I sure didn't. And it took me a long time to figure it out. I was picked on in school, but not for being gay. It was for being too quiet and shy. I was honest to a fault, and it was difficult for me to defend myself. Boys found me an easy target for torment, and girls didn't like me either. I found out the girls thought I was a snob because I rarely spoke to anyone. I thought it was obvious how terrified, lonely, and subhuman I felt. But today my partner and I can walk around town holding hands and not think anything of it. Not everyone can do that yet, but it's possible for more gay people than ever before.

1975
Saint Louis, Missouri

reidar, age 7

This is a photo of me on my seventh birthday. I loved my Big Josh doll; he was a friend of the Big Jim doll. Even though I had no idea what being gay meant back then, I knew I really liked that Big Josh doll a lot. I guess the butch boys would call him an "action figure."

1960   1970   1980   1990

1976
Spearman, Texas

trent, age 4

Growing up Southern Baptist, I was taught that being gay was bad. My mom thought gay people were mythical beings, "like werewolves or vampires," she once said. One time at dinner, when my parents found out I went to a drag show with my then-girlfriend, my father told me he used to go to gay clubs to "beat the shit out of the fags."

I am only officially out to one of my sisters, but six years ago my mom saw that my MySpace profile status listed me as gay. She sent me a long e-mail asking what she had done wrong as a mother, saying that she couldn't believe her eyes. She hasn't spoken of it since. And I'm sure she didn't share the news with anyone else.

After two suicide attempts, I moved to Los Angeles to reclaim my life. Today, I have a great boyfriend and I couldn't be happier. I still don't share anything about my personal life with my family. Considering how religious and conservative they all are, it's the best course of action. However, they all have this photo of me, so I'm sure that in their hearts they all know I was born this way.

1960   1970   1980   1990

1976
Derby, England,
United Kingdom

chris, age 5

I grew up in a tough neighborhood, but that didn't
deter me from doing the things I wanted to do, in
spite of much disapproval. I chose all my own clothes
and insisted on walking around dressed like a young
aristocrat. A favorite game of mine was pretending
to be Miss Piggy, Wonder Woman, or one of Charlie's
Angels, as I hoped to be powerful like them when I
grew up. I was a reflective, quiet child who loved to read
and make up stories. I hated sports and getting dirty.
Other children made fun of me because I wouldn't play
football or rough games. I often sat quietly alone on
the playground, and I never understood why people
disapproved of me so much. Adults despaired at what
they considered bizarre tastes for a boy, and they
made their disdain known. My father disapproved
of my desire to have a dollhouse, so I learned to keep
quiet around him. In high school some of my teachers
picked on me, so I learned to keep to myself. Yet I grew
stronger as I got older, and I gained acceptance by
hanging about with other boys who were similar to me.
I came out at school when I was fifteen, and although
it was no surprise to anyone, I wasn't readily accepted.
I weathered it all and came through the other side alive
and well.

pierre, age 5

My photo was taken inside our cabin in Saint-Donat, Quebec. It was Christmas morning, and I'd just woken up, very excited to get all my gifts. I sat down beside the fireplace, and **my mother couldn't believe my pose!** She asked me not to move, grabbed her camera, and took the shot. I have amazing parents who always **showed me how to be a great person** and to embrace whatever makes us all different.

1977
Saint-Donat,
Quebec,
Canada

david, age 7

Looking at this snapshot now makes me laugh. It's a little embarrassing remembering my habit of licking my lips, turning my head to one side, and squinting just before every picture because **I thought it made me look mysterious.** But it's a habit that paid off years later in the bars when I was learning how to cruise. I came out when I was twenty-three years old. My effort at being straight—marriage and child—failed miserably, and **I didn't see the point in lying anymore.** It wasn't a perfect coming-out experience by any means, but we all survived.

1960   1970   1980   1990

emanuel, age 6

My stepfather used to refer to me as *mariconcito* behind my mom's back. That's Spanish slang for "little faggot," and at this age, **I was probably just beginning to understand that it was not a good thing.**

My mom was responsible for dressing me up in these cutesy little outfits. This teddy bear was my best friend, and I didn't go anywhere without him. I'm pretty sure everyone picked up on my effeminate ways. Sadly, the religious influence and machismo of my Latino culture made me out to be deserving of much abuse. Nonetheless, I grew up to become a successful writer and turned all of that childhood adversity into fodder for art.

I would encourage queer youth to embrace whatever creative talents they may have and express themselves through music, painting, literature, or whatever gets them through. **Sometimes those of us who have been emotionally crippled are capable of creating great art and contributing to the inspiration of others.** Even if you create it just for yourself. it's great for letting go of hurt and moving on in life.

1960   1970   1980   1990

jeffrey, age 8

My folks lovingly tolerated my fascination with Dracula.
All that Vaseline in my hair was pretty hard to wash out,
but it was worth it! I certainly wasn't conscious of it at the
time, but there was something about this dark, hypnotic,
dominating masculine figure that must have struck a
chord with me. Dracula routinely wreaked havoc on
normal society, and even if he was destroyed in the end,
he was just doing what came naturally to him. Was he
appealing to me because I innately knew I was different
as well? My Dracula obsession branded me a weirdo,
which was good preparation for becoming comfortable
with my own difference. I got a head start in accepting
my own outsider status, and I found it empowering to be
considered a bit of a freak among my peers.

chris, age 2

I always felt like a fabulous fish out of water in my hometown. This picture fairly screams "gay." It was taken in the days of disco, when I enjoyed playing with dolls, banging on the piano, and looking like a young, gay version of Hugh Hefner. If I'd known when this photo was taken, I would have told myself that everything would be okay once I grew up and moved away! There was a lot of the world out there to see. And after I saw some of it, I got to appreciate where I came from, as well as who I am and have always been.

1977
East Grand
Forks,
Minnesota

1960   1970   1980   1990

1978
Adelaide,
South
Australia,
Australia

sia, age 3

As a little girl, I didn't really mind if you were a boy
or a girl. **I just wanted you to love me!** Honestly, it
wasn't until a few years ago that I really realized I was
queer. Now, I call myself an art fag, a lezzie, a dyke, and
straight. But the truth is, labels don't matter.

1960   1970   1980   1990

1979

Pawling, New York

bill, age 14

I've been a music junkie since before I could walk. **The 45-rpm single of Shirley Ellis's "The Clapping Song" shaped me.** There are family stories of me hoisting myself up to the stereo so I could stare at the records spinning around and around. I was encouraged to be creative, and **I'm sure my parents suspected I was different.** Unfortunately, I spent most of my teenage years distancing myself from them, because I simply didn't know how to communicate the cravings that my body and mind were manifesting.

I started to come out in college. At the same time, **I was drawn to the alternative music and culture of the era.** I obsessed about bands like the Smiths, Siouxsie and the Banshees, Kate Bush, and The B-52s, devouring magazines like *Trouser Press* and *After Dark*, road-tripping from our tidy suburb to classic Manhattan dance clubs like the Ritz, Pyramid, Boy Bar, Save the Robots, and Danceteria. My house-music cherry was popped at the legendary Paradise Garage.

If only I could go back and tell the young me not to worry so much about what everyone else thinks about him. I would tell little Bill to embrace his inner joy and that it's okay to celebrate, feel free, and love unconditionally!

◆

clinton, age 13

Granted, it was the 1970s and clothes were a bit more
flamboyant, but I had a boy's haircut, a boy's name, and
I wore white tube socks, for God's sake! "Girlboy" and
"Fruit Loop" were just two of the nicknames I accrued in
my early years.

One summer day we went to a family reunion. I wore a
sleeveless blue terry-cloth T-shirt with matching shorts. I
thought it to be a "safe" and "butch" choice, since I always
wore it with sneakers and tube socks, not my beloved
flip-flops. (I'll have you know I wore flip-flops back
when no boy would be caught dead in flip-flops! You're
welcome!) We arrived at Aunt Anna and Uncle Adam's
home, and just as Aunt Anna started making the family
reintroductions, Uncle Adam, who had been ogling me
from behind his Coke-bottle spectacles, pointed at me and
asked, "And who is this lovely young lady?" Beat...beat...
awkward silence...polite laughter. Sweet Aunt Anna did
her best to cover for him: "Oh, Uncle Adam, he's as blind
as a bat." Yeah, well, was the old man so blind he couldn't
see my tube socks?!?

Looking at this photo, taken just after that awful moment,
I can see how much I wanted to disappear! But it's hard
to believe I once wanted to hide from the very thing that
put me in the spotlight. You see, I am a Girlboy! A Fruit
Loop! And I've made a career out of it! What I wouldn't
give nowadays to have someone look at me and ask, "And
who is this lovely young lady?"

1979

Bronx, New York

fernando, age 4

I feel very proud of the courage it took for me to stand
up for what I believed in, and to dare to come out at age
twenty-three in conservative and Catholic upper-class
Mexico City. At the beginning, the process of coming out
seemed painful and nearly impossible. I felt as if I'd be
the only homosexual my friends and family would ever
have to deal with. Pretty soon after I started the coming-
out process, I realized that wasn't the case. I had the
support of my friends and family, but it took a little time
for them to accept me. And, to my huge surprise, my three
closest childhood friends turned out to be gay as well. So
it's no wonder we remained friends all these years!

1979
Mexico City,
Mexico

1960   1970   1980   1990

sarah, age 4

For this kindergarten photo, I told the photographer I wanted a "serious picture." The more he tried to make me smile, the more serious I got. **And I did not like this dress.** I wanted to wear my fireman's hat, which I was usually allowed to do, since my parents weren't really invested in any particular gender expression. I love this picture because of its emotional honesty: I'm not smiling because **I don't feel like smiling.** No one was going to push me into feeling or doing something I didn't want. This is harder to accomplish as an adult, but it's always my goal.

1960   1970   1980   1990

1980
Goldsboro, North Carolina

gary & larry, age 5

We were always happy kids. When you have a twin, you've always got a playmate. We grew up Southern Baptist and went to church three times a week, so we were around constant messages that gay people were sinners who were going to burn in the lake of fire. We both just butched it up, took girls to proms and Christmas dances, and put up a front. In our small town, we couldn't be true to who we really were. We didn't tell each other about being gay until we were seventeen, so before that, each of us just kept it our own secret for fear of being rejected—not only by each other, but also by our mother. We finally came out to our parents when we were twenty-five. Our dad is slowly coming around, but our mom still has issues with us being gay. Even with all the acclaim and awards for our film (*From Hollywood to Dollywood* documents our coming-out story and journey to meet our idol), she can't stand behind it or our message. But we still love our parents unconditionally.

gabor, age 11

In this photo, I'm wearing my mother's dress and sun hat and parading around our house. My father was a scientist and my mother was a pianist, and they were progressive and bohemian European nudists. They had gay people in their circle of friends, so **while I was at home, I felt safe.** It wasn't until I started middle school that the bullying and torture began over my sexuality. And I quickly learned that I had better start hiding my truth, to avoid physical and emotional attacks, many of which led me to the brink of suicide. In this photograph, **I am still happy and free,** like so many of the childhood photos in this book. Many of these pictures capture us as **the joy-filled spirits** we once were, before the mean world forced us to change. Today, I feel lucky and free again.

1970　　　　1980　　　　1990　　　　2000

diana, age 4

In this photo, I'm trying to ride my father's Vespa. Needless to say, I still ride motorcycles today. **I have always been a tomboy,** and luckily my parents didn't do anything to change that. I'm thankful for my genes every day. Just **be authentic,** and people will love you in spite of their prejudice.

1980
Verona, Italy

1970   1980   1990   2000

glen, age 11

The 1980s were a challenging decade for coming out, as the news of a "gay cancer" was at its peak. My parents could not understand what AIDS meant. They told me, "They should take all the gays and people who are infected with HIV and drop them on a secluded island." I was devastated. I left home at a young age, joined the military, got married, and had kids. It didn't work. I officially came out at age twenty-six to a still very unsupportive family. My parents disowned me. But I realized that if they didn't accept me, I had to be happy by myself. And I'm okay with that, because I know that I was born this way.

1981
El Paso, Texas

1970   1980   1990   2000

donald, age 11

**Only a young gay boy could strike a pose with a five-
pound carp!** I enjoyed playing in the dirt, climbing trees,
fishing, and doing archery. I was not into girly stuff, even
when my two older sisters dressed me up in pigtails and
paraded me around the neighborhood. The word *gay*
didn't enter my vocabulary until about seven years ago,
when I figured out that I was gay—after being married
for seven years and having two absolutely wonderful
sons. I sometimes wonder: Did my mom know all along?
I look at this photo now and just **wish I could be that
naive and unafraid boy again.** It is so important to get
over the fear of simply being you.

1970   1980   1990   2000

1981
San Dimas,
California

tommy, age 7

Here I'm wearing my favorite shirt from the second grade. I called it my Star Wars Lando Calrissian shirt because it was breezy. But the best part was that only the top had a real button; the rest were snaps. My best friend and I played *Dukes of Hazzard* at recess. I always played Bo Duke, and he ripped my shirt open during fight scenes. After that he would kick my butt, and I would make him play Daisy Duke to nurse me back to health. Some boys came up one day and said we couldn't play like that, because Daisy was a girl. My friend decided we'd play with them, and one boy who didn't know how to properly rip open a snap-up shirt actually ripped my shirt. I had to sit through class for the rest of the day in that ripped shirt while other kids giggled and called me Daisy—despite the fact that I was clearly Bo. When I told my mom how my shirt got ripped, she gave me one of those looks where I could sense something had changed between us. Needless to say, she refused to buy me another snap-up shirt for school. But years later, my mom sent my first boyfriend and me matching snap-up shirts for Christmas. And I think my boyfriend ended up ripping that one, too.

aaron, age 8

I think this picture is funny because I'm so excited about my pink Easter basket—much more excited than my younger sister Denise. Growing up in a small town in Indiana, I always knew I was different from other boys. I had a very high voice all through puberty, and I was so androgynous that it was hard for people to tell whether I was a boy or a girl. I remember having a huge crush on my swimming instructor. All through grade school, I much preferred playing with the girls on the playground instead of anything involving a ball. I was a boy soprano until eighth grade, then an alto as a freshman.

Today, my wonderful family accepts my partner and me. They are fundamental Christians who will never approve of me being gay, but they do accept and love me. Most of the people you're afraid to tell that you're gay already know. They're just waiting for you to be comfortable enough with yourself to approach them with it. It's generally not a surprise to anyone. It's okay to wait until you're comfortable to have a conversation about it. Move at your own pace.

1970   1980   1990   2000

1982
Berne, Indiana

sutan, age 7

Growing up in Bali, Indonesia, **I loved watching the folk dancers with their gilded costumes and bright colors.** My older sister, who was quite a tomboy, was taking traditional dance lessons, and I remember being more interested in the instruction than she was. I would stand behind her and the teacher, emulating all the stomps, finger wiggling, and eye moves. My parents tell stories about how I would turn a box into a stage and perform for them at three years old! My favorite thing to do was find my own little corner, with tons of blankets, sheets, and odd and ends. I'd spend hours making costumes and putting on shows, which was far more interesting than kicking a ball around the playground. **I remember being called names in school at a young age, and people had to explain to me what those words meant.** I don't think I realized I was gay until someone else pointed it out to me. In my early teens, we moved to California, and I discovered all the old classic movies. I'd watch *The King and I* and *Singing in the Rain*. All these things that influenced me are still my favorites today, except now my friends call my private play space my own "Genie Bottle."

jarryd, age 3

When I came across this photo in a family album, the first thing that came to my mind was, "Oh, the crazy '80s!" Check out the mohair sofa and wood paneling. (Obviously this was a truly dark time for interior design.) That said, it's time the world knows that I would've kept that handbag if I'd realized how truly fierce I looked with it. And the storage inside was amazing! I mean, that bag carried all my necessities: sunglasses, ChapStick, breath mints, and, of course, My Little Pony. You can't see it in the photo, but I totally had my nails painted pink pearl. I thank my grandmother for that—I wanted them painted, and she did them for me. Many gay people say, "Growing up I always knew." As a kid, it wasn't just me who knew. Everyone knew I was different. I was lucky enough to have a family who supported me right from the start and never once tried to hold me back.

1983

Loveland, Ohio

1970   1980   1990   2000

perez, age 5

When I look at my childhood photos, I remember those times fondly. I had a normal and happy upbringing. I was six years old when I first became aware that I was gay. I was too young to realize exactly what my feelings meant, but I knew I was attracted to guys. At school I felt like an outsider, but thankfully I found like-minded individuals I could be friends with. We were involved in plays and drama club and I found a great sense of community there, so I never felt lonely or sad growing up. **Strangely enough, I was never a victim of homophobia,** but I was a victim of fat-phobia. I was picked on for being fat rather than being gay.

After high school I left Miami to study at NYU where it seemed everybody was out and proud. After a semester, I decided it was time to tell my mom the truth about my sexuality. Although my mom was accepting, she wasn't glowingly receptive of the news. **It's difficult for any parent to understand that their child is going against what the world views as "normal."** Over the years, my mom has become more accepting of my sexuality, and our relationship could not be better right now. Being gay has become easier over the years. When I was growing up there weren't many gay role models on TV. Today the media is filled with positive examples. I'm also privileged that I am viewed as a successful individual who happens to be gay, and that I can be who I am without judgment.

1970   1980   1990   2000

1983

Miami, Florida

paul, age 4

My childhood dream was to be Snow White. Although I couldn't whistle, I regaled everyone with my versions of "Whistle While You Work" and "Some Day My Prince Will Come," raising some eyebrows around the house. I also started channeling my creative energy into another outlet: drawing. My parents sought the mentorship of a local artist who took me under her wing when I was four years old. She taught me that anything I imagined could come to life on canvas. Soon, every wall in our house was covered with oil-painted tributes to my favorite heroines. Then I decided that I didn't want to be Snow White when I grew up; I wanted to be an artist. I'm grateful that I had a mentor who cared enough to fan this creative flame, because the other flaming aspects of my personality presented problems at school. Boys with high-pitched voices whose approach to running in gym class could be described as "prancing" didn't fare well. I learned that, in order to survive, I had to conceal those aspects of my personality. But I wasn't able to describe what I was covering up as gay yet. That didn't hit me until right after college. My fairy tale has a very happy ending: I found my way out of the dark enchanted forest to a place of self-acceptance. I even found my own handsome prince, and our life together is as close to "happily ever after" as I can imagine.

1984
Grove City, Ohio

shannon, age 6

Here I am in costume before **my very first dance recital**.
I was thrilled. When kids on the bus found out I took
dance lessons, they'd sing Lionel Ritchie's "Ballerina
Girl" to mock me. I had so much closeted shame
back then. But **I still wanted to perform and feel the
tremendous joy** I felt when I was dancing on stage.

1970   1980   1990   2000

brian, age 5

My obsession with He-Man and the Masters of the Universe began at age four. My mother introduced me to She-Ra and then bought me this Crystal Castle play set for my fifth birthday—even though those toys were marketed for girls. Years later, she explained that she knew I was gay at an early age when I quoted the appropriately titled Masters of the Universe episode "The Rainbow Warrior": "A mother always knows her own son. And I've always been very proud of you."

1985
Machesney Park, Illinois

1970   1980   1990   2000

noah, age 7

At age five, I crept out to my front yard in just my Scooby Doo Underoos and did a dance for our insanely good-looking garbage man. When I came back inside I proudly announced to my dad that the garbage man called me a "queer." My father immediately jumped up, ready to confront the man who had spit such an offensive word at his little boy. Before my dad could turn the doorknob, I stopped him and explained that I didn't mind being a queer. Of course, I had no idea what *queer* meant in that context. I thought it merely meant I was strange and unusual, something I thought I wanted to be back then. I soon learned that being a queer wasn't something you should wish for, after the taunting and tormenting I suffered at the hands of my classmates. I was pushed down a flight of stairs as a freshman in high school. Luckily, I had an amazing family to escape to after a day of terror in school. But I realize that not everyone is as fortunate. Today, when I hear about kids coming out at the ages of fourteen or twelve or nine, I'm shocked and amazed. I salute those kids, marvel at their bravery, wish them only good things, and hope that the trend continues until it's no longer a trend and we finally realize that queer kids really are just born this way.

1985
Racine, Wisconsin

lindsay, age 3

As a tomboy, I spent much of my childhood with my cousin Russ, who's the same age as me. Russ's older brother taught us new words like *fag* and *queerbait*, and I have a vivid memory of Russ actually calling me *gay* at age six. I asked him what it meant, and he said, "It means you're a girl that likes girls." **I took a moment to process that in my little brain and I concluded, "Yeah, you're right."**

seth, age 10

This was a weekend game night at my mom's house. I was always trying to entertain my family with my best supermodel pose, way before the age of supermodels. The terry-cloth hot pants still kill me! They were my everyday shorts; all the other clothing was my mom's. I also remember that this was the first time my older brother—whom I idolized—called me a fag. **The hardest part of being called names like that was knowing they were right.** I couldn't prove them wrong. And it really created a sense of doom inside me. That feeling lasted until I finally got out of Virginia at age eighteen and began to live my life.

1985
Fredericksburg, Virginia

1970   1980   1990   2000

eva, age 3

Coming out as a lesbian was as difficult for me as it is for any gay kid. But the fact that I am physically disabled and nonverbal made it a bit harder, and I have to use a letter board to spell out my thoughts. Imagine the stress of slowly coming out, letter by letter. On top of that, I didn't have any gay disabled role models to look up to, and I felt very alone. Fortunately, when I did come out, my family and friends were totally cool. I'm pretty sure they'd all figured it out by then anyway. Now, as an adult, I embrace my queerness and consider it just one more aspect that makes me unique.

1986
Los Angeles, California

1970   1980   1990   2000

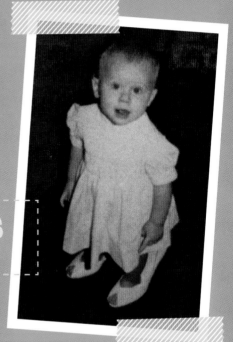

heather, age 1

The baby in this photo is now a successful, high-heel-wearing, twenty-five-year-old lipstick lesbian. My parents, who disowned me when I came out three years ago, have missed out on a lot of my life. But I wouldn't go back into the closet for *anything*. After all, how would all my shoes and purses fit in there with me?

1970　　　　　　1980　　　　　　1990　　　　　　2000

kyle, age 3

I was always some version of different as a child: different as in smart, different as in social, different as in gay. I rehearsed Michael Jackson dance routines at age four and memorized a graduate microbiology textbook at age five. I knew I was gay at age twelve, though my peers had been letting me know long before that. My dad understood how hard things were in high school, and he added thirty minutes to his commute each morning to take me to school, so I wouldn't have to ride the bus. To avoid the bullies, I walked from class to class outside and picked seats near the exits.

You must be your own advocate. Whatever pain or disillusionment you experience must be redirected, or it will weigh you down. Be fiercely loyal to your friends, and never let someone project their inadequacies onto you. **Love unconditionally and try to be kind.**

1970   1980   1990   2000

shawn, age 5

This is way back in my childhood in Ohio. Rural Ohio. *Very* rural Ohio. A neighborhood girl pressured me into a marriage of convenience with the words, "Hey, let's play getting married!" **My mom baked a Duncan Hines cake, and her older brother played preacher.** We said our wedding vows, had an awkward kiss, stuffed our faces with cake, and then danced on the porch. Seeing this photograph again makes me realize how effeminate I've always been. **It makes me wonder why anyone would ever want to make me feel bad about being *fabulous*!**

1987
Litchfield, Ohio

1970　　　　1980　　　　1990　　　　2000

matt, age 7

Always an overachiever, I can be seen here (at *right*)
demonstrating not one but two limp wrists. This level of
fabulous has clearly blinded my brother. Even at seven
years old, I was already telling other kids that I was gay.
I didn't know what it meant, but I knew it was bad and
won me lots of attention. The fact that it got me negative
attention didn't matter. Around age fifteen, I realized,
"Oh, wait—I really am gay." For a while, I just wanted
to hide from it. But that seven-year-old pride parade in
my heart couldn't be stifled. By eleventh grade, I'd made
a promise to myself that if anyone asked, I'd be honest.
Unfortunately, my schoolmates decided that the ideal
time to ask me was in the locker room during gym class.
"Why do you wear nail polish?" someone demanded.
"Ummmmm…" I said. "Are you gay?" they continued.
"Uh…yes, but that's not why I wear polish," I replied.
I think this particular nuance was lost in the ensuing
bedlam. These days I work as a journalist in San
Francisco, writing for one of the country's oldest LGBTQ
newspapers, and I document the fight for marriage
equality online. My husband and I have been together
for ten years, and my parents, my brother, his wife, and
the entire clan all welcome and love him. That little
seven-year-old inside me is still running around telling
everyone that I'm gay with absolutely no reservations.

1987
Southington, Connecticut

clint, age 5

After I told my closest friends, I sat my entire extended
family down at Thanksgiving and simply said, "I am
gay." The reply from the crowd was, "So? We love you
for *you*."

1970   1980   1990   2000

melissa, age 6

I remember thinking I was a boy, seeing no difference between me and other boys. It wasn't until puberty that I realized I was indeed a girl, and that sent my world into upheaval. But once I met other gay people in high school, I finally understood that I wasn't different or weird. I was just queer. And that was awesome!

ken, age 8

My parents and I spent the summer of 1989 with my mom's cousins in California. Thirteen years later, my mom told the same cousins that her son was gay. "We knew since he was a little kid," they replied. "You didn't know?" **My relationship with my mom got so much better after I came out to her.** It took her a few months to digest the news. But soon enough, **she was telling all her close friends and relatives all about me.**

1970   1980   1990   2000

kyan, age 4

At this age, I didn't realize that I was gay—although I imagine others around me suspected. It wasn't until late elementary school, around age eleven, that I started to become aware. As time went on, the Internet helped me make it through, by connecting me with other gay men around the globe. Eventually, the media provided me with great outlets to understand that **life for a gay man could be great.** *Queer as Folk* became one of my favorite shows during high school.

Working through these feelings was far from easy, especially growing up in rural West Virginia, where the redneck-and-Republican-to-homosexual ratios are greatly skewed. My mother frequently reminded me that gays would burn in hell. Fortunately, my mom has since become very supportive.

1989
Ripley, West Virginia

1970   1980   1990   2000

kevin, age 7

In this photo, you'll notice I had all of four teeth. For some reason, my adult teeth took forever to grow in, leaving me with the thickest lisp possible; thus, I thounded like the gayeth little boy in the whole thcool. It also didn't help that I wore that same mock turtleneck every day, like it was a full-time job. Things got so bad that my school sent me to speech class for three years—a class they created just for me.

I remember an obsession with swords at this time in my life. Why? So I could pretend to be She-Ra, of course. Never He-Man. But nobody could make out the fact that I was saying, "By the power of Grayskull!" To this day, my family still teases me about shouting, "Baw-dee-aw-nees of Graythkull!" In retrospect, it all worked out really well. I grew up from a little lisping gay boy into a big gay man.

1980   1990   2000   2010

kurt, age 5

I'm Kurt on the left with my (also gay) twin brother Matt on the right. I didn't fully realize that I was gay until middle school. But I wasn't ready to admit it to anyone, including myself, until I was a senior in high school.

When I stumbled upon this picture at my dad's house, my first thought was, "How did you all *not* know that we were gay?" Especially when we spent so much time playing Cinderella and adoring our purple My Little Pony dolls? My brother and I have been really lucky to have a supportive family and great friends. Perhaps if we'd stayed in the Mormon church, things would've been different. But we stopped attending around eight years old, and we haven't looked back. Growing up, I never thought that if I came out, my mom would be saying things like, "You should go talk to that cute gay guy at Starbucks." But she really does.

1990

Springfield,
Oregon

eamonn, age 4

To me, girls always made such fabulous friends that I
couldn't conceive of being with them romantically. I was
in third grade when I first learned what *gay* meant. By
age twelve, I decided that gay was the way I planned
to live the rest of my life—and with someone tall, dark,
strong, and handsome!

1980   1990   2000   2010

ernesto, age 6

My teen years were full of angst and could be perfectly narrated by Christina Ricci. I was a little lonesome, with no gay peers. Then high school came, and I began to embrace my homosexuality. I would no longer awkwardly dodge the "Are you gay?" question and I began to taste my freedom.

Today my favorite color is blue, my favorite animal is a lion (although some would argue it's a bear), and my favorite game is Scrabble. And my favorite holiday is still Valentine's Day.

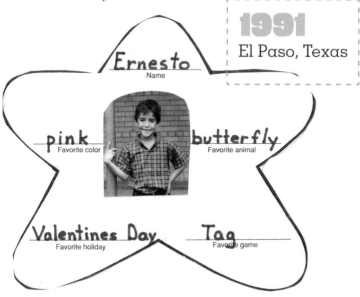

1991
El Paso, Texas

Ernesto
Name

pink
Favorite color

butterfly
Favorite animal

Valentines Day
Favorite holiday

Tag
Favorite game

reese, age 5

I remember having a crush on a classmate named Dustin, and I remember how hard I cried when he moved away just before the start of first grade. I also remember my love of the hand-on-hip pose, as is evident in this photo. If anything, **looking back on pictures of me like this makes me remember how unselfconscious I was.**

Once I hit fifth grade, everything changed. That's when the bullying started, and the name-calling, and getting my butt kicked after school: all those terrible things that so many of us have to deal with as gay kids. My parents were always supportive of me, but one memory in particular sticks out as the first moment that my mother truly offered her love and support. One night when I was about seven years old, we were watching *Melrose Place* together. There was a gay character on the show (a doctor portrayed by Doug Savant), and in one episode he kisses another man, or it's implied that they've had sex or something. I remember when the episode ended and the credits were rolling, my mom turned to me and said, **"Reese, that character is gay. And that's okay."**

1991

Bellingham,
Washington

lisa, age 8

This picture sparks many awkward, depressing memories of never fitting in with my perfect, happy friends or my strict Mormon family. I had just convinced my mother to let me cut my long hair. It traumatized me. Since then, I've vowed to make myself look as feminine as possible.

The first time I remember having a real girl crush was at age thirteen. I'd doodled on a piece of paper about loving a girl, and my sister told my mom. When confronted, I cried, "Nooo! I don't love her like *that*, just as a friend!" But that was when I realized I was different, and there was something about me I was supposed to be ashamed of. I soon moved myself back into the closet and locked the door from the inside.

Although being gay and Mormon is hard, when I start to feel sad I hear a voice inside my head saying, "God doesn't make mistakes." And I feel content. I've been blessed with an amazing family that loves me and supports me, no matter what.

1993
Mesa, Arizona

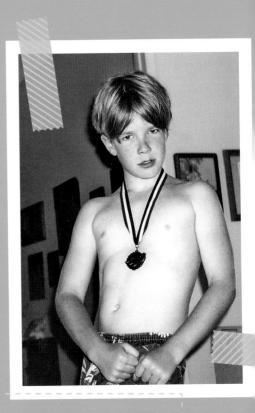

1995
Los Angeles, California

joshua, age 12

I had a bumpy childhood, raised by a single mother suffering from multiple personality disorder. My best friend knew I was in love with him, and he was okay with that. as long as I didn't "try anything funny." I bounced around foster homes and group homes until I was fifteen. That was when I came out, and it was the best decision I have ever made. After I came out everyone was so kind and loving toward me.

Today I'm a professional ballet dancer, and I've been partnered with my husband and best friend for seven years. I'm currently attending grad school and making a documentary that follows a group of LGBTQ kids in their early teens, to give a voice to the younger generation who are experiencing these things. I love being gay. and I wouldn't want to be any other way. I hope my film helps kids come to that place of acceptance in life a lot sooner than I did. Someday, being young and gay will be as taboo as being young and short or having freckles. And I want to make that day come very soon.

1995

Auckland, New Zealand

andrew, age 8

I picked the fabric for this vest myself. And **I felt fabulous in rainbow houndstooth,** as I'm sure any other eight-year-old at his father's fortieth birthday party would have felt—right?

My dad dreaded picking me up from preschool because **I'd always be wearing some frilly outfit from the playtime box.** I didn't realize I was gay until much later, mostly because I didn't know being gay was possible! I grew up in a sheltered Christian home, and everyone just thought I was "special."

Coming out was hard for me. **I was twenty-one, I had just met the love of my life, and I knew I couldn't keep him to myself.** It was awful for a few months because my family was shocked beyond belief. Of course, nobody else was. My family and I have been able to slip into a "don't ask, don't tell" kind of understanding. My partner, Paul, and I have been together for three years now. Mathieu, my best friend since birth (who's pictured with me), is soon getting married and I'll be his best man. **Someday I hope that he can be the best man at my wedding, too.** As the world becomes more accepting, that just might be possible.

matthew, age 5

I wore this outfit to the park with my family, and some boys made fun of me. I was so upset, I never wore it again. That broke my mother's heart. She didn't like seeing me feel uncomfortable trying to be myself or doing things I wanted to do. I'm proud of my parents for buying that fairy outfit for me when I asked for it. But it also makes me sad that so many children can't innocently express themselves, simply because they might not fit our societally defined roles.

1995
London, England, United Kingdom

1980   1990   2000   2010

1998
Limerick,
Ireland

michelle, age 5

I never chose to be anything. I was just a carefree
little gay Irish girl from day one.

1980   1990   2000   2010

are you proud to say that you were born this way?